Volume I

CONTEN

Music setting and arrangement by John Canning
Illustrations courtesy of Peter Stubbs

Order No. 11AWAL-1348
ISBN No. 1 978-1-85720-182-6

Exclusive Distributors:
Waltons Publishing, Unit 6A, Rosemount Park Drive, Rosemount Business Park,
Ballycoolin Road, Blanchardstown, Dublin 11, Ireland
Walton Music Inc., P.O. Box 874, New York, NY 10009, U.S.A.

1 3 5 7 9 0 8 6 4 2

Be Kind to Auld Grannie

Words by Archibald Mackay, a bookbinder from Kilmarnock, and author of a small volume of songs called *Ingleside Lilts*, which means fireside lilts. The music is by T.S. Gleadhill.

Arrangement copyright Waltons Publishing

Be kind to auld gran-nie for noo she is frail, As a time shat-ter'd tree bend-ing low in the gale, When you were wee bair-nies tot tot-ting a-bout, She watch'd ye when in, and she watch'd ye when out, And aye when ye chanc'd in yer daf-fin and fun To dunt yer wee heads on the cauld stan-ney grun', She lift-ed ye up and she kissed ye full fain, Till a' yer bit cares were for-got-ten a-gain, Then be kind to auld gran-nie for noo she is frail As a time shat-ter'd tree bend ing low in the gale.

When first in your breasts rose that feeling divine,
That's wak'd by the tales and the sangs o' lang syne,
Wi' auld-warld cracks she would pleasure inspire,
In the lang winter nights as she sat by the fire;
Or melt your young hearts wi' some sweet Scottish lay,
Like 'Flow'rs o' the Forest' or 'Auld Robbie Gray';
Though eerie the win' blew around our bit cot,
Grim winter and a' its wild blasts were forgot;
Then be kind to auld grannie, for noo she is frail,
As a time shatter'd tree bending low in the gale.

And mind though the blythe day o' youth is noo yours,
Time will wither its joys, as wild winter the flow'rs;
And your step that's noo licht as the bound o' the roe,
Wi' cheerless auld age may be feeble and slow;
And the frien's o' your youth to the grave may be gane,
And ye on its brink may be tott'ring alane;
Oh, think how consoling some frien' would be then,
When the gloaming o' life comes like mist o'er the glen;
Then be kind to auld grannie, for noo she is frail,
As a time shatter'd tree bending low in the gale.

Coulter's Candy

Coulter was Robert Coltart, who sold his home-made candy round the Borders
in the early part of the twentieth century.

Arrangement copyright Waltons Publishing

Al - ly, bal - ly, al - ly bal - ly bee, Sit- tin' on yer mam- my's knee

Gree- tin' for a - ni- ther baw- bee, Tae buy mair Coul- ter's can - dy.

Dinna you greet, my wee babby,
You know your daddy's gone to sea,
Earnin' pennies for you and me
To buy some Coulter's candy.

Mammy gie me ma thrifty doon,
Here's auld Coulter comin' roon.
He's been roon' aboot the toon
Singin' and sellin' candy.

Little Annie's greetin' tae,
Sae whit can puir wee Mammy dae?
But gie them a penny atween them twae
Tae buy mair Coulter's Candy.

Poor wee Jeannie's lookin' affa thin,
A rickle o' banes covered ower wi' skin,
Noo she's gettin' a double chin
Wi' sookin' Coulter's Candy.

Farewell tae Tarwathie

Words by George Scroggie.

Arrangement copyright Waltons Publishing

Fare - weel tae Tar - wa - thie, a - dieu Mor - mond Hill, And the dear land o' Cri-mond I bid ye fare - well, I am bound out for Green-land and rea-dy to sail, In hopes to find rich - es in hun-ting the whale.

Adieu to my comrades, for awhile we must part,
And likewise the dear lass that fair won my heart;
The cold ice of Greenland, my love will not chill,
And the longer my absence, more loving she'll feel.

Our ship is well rigged and she's ready to sail,
Our crew, they are anxious to follow the whale,
Where the icebergs do float and the stormy winds blow,
Where the land and the ocean are covered with snow.

The cold coast of Greenland is barren and bare,
No seed time nor harvest is ever known there,
And the birds here sing sweetly on mountain and dale,
But there is nae a birdie to sing tae the whale.

There is no habitation for a man to live there,
And the king of that country is the fierce Greenland bear,
And there is no temptation to tarry long there,
Wi' our ship bumper full, we will homeward repair.

So farewell tae Tarwathie, adieu Mormond Hill
And the dear land o' Crimond, I'll bid you fareweel,
I'm bound out for Greenland and ready to sail,
In hopes to find riches in hunting the whale.

Green Grow the Rashes O

Words by Robert Burns set to an older "not quite polite song".

Arrangement copyright Waltons Publishing

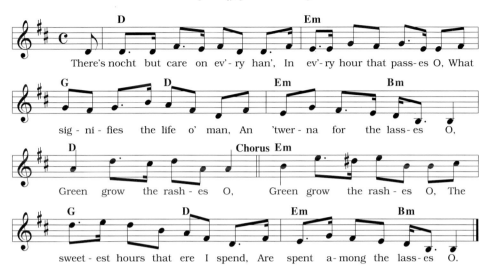

There's nocht but care on ev'-ry han', In ev'-ry hour that pass-es O, What sig-ni-fies the life o' man, An 'twer-na for the lass-es O, Green grow the rash-es O, Green grow the rash-es O, The sweet-est hours that ere I spend, Are spent a-mong the lass-es O.

The warldly race may riches chase,
An' riches still may fly them, O,
An' though at last they catch them fast,
Their hearts can ne'er enjoy them, O,
   Chorus

Gie me a cannie hour at e'en
My arms around my dearie, O,
An' warldly cares, an' warldly men
May a' gae tapsalteerie, O,
   Chorus

An' you sae douce, wha sneer at this
Ye're naught but senseless asses, O,
The wisest man the world e'er saw,
He dearly lo'ed the lasses, O,
   Chorus

Auld nature swears the lovely dears,
Her noblest wark she classes, O,
Her 'prentice han' she tried on man,
And then she made the lasses, O.
   Chorus

Come o'er the Stream Charlie

Words by James Hogg (1770-1835). The tune is "MacLean's Welcome".

Arrangement copyright Waltons Publishing

Come o'er the stream, Char-lie, dear Char-lie, brave Char-lie, Come o'er the stream, Char-lie, and dine with Mac-Lean. And though you be wea-ry, we'll make your heart chee-ry, And wel-come our Char-lie and his loy-al train. We'll bring down the red deer, we'll bring down the black steer, The lamb from the brac-ken, and doe from the glen; The salt sea we'll har-ry, and bring to our Char-lie The cream of our bo-thy, and curd from the pen.

Chorus

And you shall drink freely
The dews of Glen Sheerly
That stream in the starlight
When kings dinna ken;
And deep be your meed
O' the wine that is red,
To drink to your sire
And his frien' the MacLean.
    Chorus

If aught will invite you,
Or more will delight you,
'Tis ready a troop
Of oor bold Hieland men
Shall range on the heather
Wi' bonnet and feather,
Strong arms and broad claymores,
Three hundred and ten.
    Chorus

The Magdalen Green

The word "Magdalen" is pronounced "maudlin" in the song.
An early Dundee Town Council record (1582) describes it as "Maidlane Geir" (*geir* being a stretch of land).

Arrangement copyright Waltons Publishing

I am a brisk, young sai-lor lad just new-ly come from sea, My
gal-lant ship lies an-chored in the har-bour o' Dun - dee, Young
Bet-sy being the fair-est girl that e'er my eyes have seen, I
asked her wid she take a walk all a-long by the Mag-dalen Green.

But, roguish smile upon her face, she answered me and said,
"To take a walk with you young man it's I would be afraid.
For the roads they are so slippery and the night so hard and keen,
And it would not do for me to fall all along the Magdalen Green."

But with false words and flattering tongue the lass soon gied consent,
We wandered here, we wandered there, and happy times we spent.
And mony's the day and night we roamed to view the pleasant scene;
I'm afraid this maid got mony's the fall all along the Magdalen Green.

But some strange thought had crossed my mind that I would go to sea,
And leave my bonny Betsy, my maid o' sweet Dundee.
I bade farewell to Dundee where happy we had been,
And left this maid to weep and mourn all along by the Magdalen Green.

One night as I lay slumbering I dreamed a fearful dream,
I dreamed I was the father of a darling little son;
And for that dear young maiden I saw her there quite plain,
And she was sad lamenting all along by the Magdalen Green.

So come all you brisk young sailor lads and a warning take by me,
Never love a fair young maid then shun her company;
But I'll come back to Dundee town, for a rascal I have been,
And I will make it up to her all along the Magdalen Green.

The Mother's Malison

Arrangement copyright Waltons Publishing

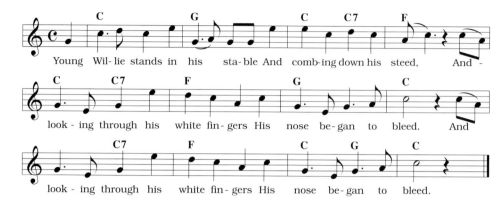

Young Wil-lie stands in his sta-ble And comb-ing down his steed, And -
look-ing through his white fin-gers His nose be-gan to bleed. And
look-ing through his white fin-gers His nose be-gan to bleed.

Bring corn, corn to my horse
And meat unto my men,
For I'm awa to Maggie's bowers
I'll win or she lie doon.
For I'm awa to Maggie's bowers
I'll win or she lie doon.

O stay, o stay this ae nicht, Willie,
O stay and dinna gang,
For there is a noise in Clyde Waters
Wid fear a thousand men.
For there is a noise in Clyde Waters
Wid fear a thousand men.

It's I've a steed in my stable
Cost me twice twenty pounds,
And I'll put trust in his forelegs
Tae carry me safe along.
And I'll put trust in his forelegs
Tae carry me safe along.

As I rode o'er yon high high hill
And down yon dreary glen,
It's o spare me, spare me, Clyde waters,
O spare me as I gang
Make me the wreck as I come back,
But spare me as I gang.

As I rode o'er yon high high hill
And down yon dreary glen,
It's I hae reached at Maggie's window,
Rise up and lat me in
For my boots are full of Clyde waters,
And I'm frozen tae the chin.

It's up arose her mother dear
A' for tae speak tae him,
"It's my stable's full of horse," she says,
"My barn's full of hay.
And my bowers are full of gentlemen,
So ye can' get in till day."

He turned his horse right round about
Wi' the saut tear in his e'e,
I never thought tae come here this nicht
And be denied by thee.
I never thought tae come here this nicht
And be denied by thee.

As he rode o'er yon high hill
And down yon dreary glen,
The rush that ran in Clyde waters
Took Willie's cane frae him.
The rush that ran in Clyde waters
Took Willie's cane frae him.

As Willie he sat saddle o'er
To catch his cane again,
The rush that ran in Clyde waters
Took Willie's hat frae him.
The rush that ran in Clyde waters
Took Willie's hat frae him.

His brother being on the other side
Cries, "Willie will ye droon?
Oh haud ye tae yer high horse heid,
He'll learn ye how to swim.
Oh haud ye tae yer high horse heid,
He'll learn ye how to swim."

O why could I turn ae my high horse heid
An' learn how to swim?
It's the deepest pot in a' the Clyde
And here that I maun droon.
It's the deepest pot in a' the Clyde
And here that I maun droon.

It's up she rose her Maggie dear
All in a frightful dream,
For she dreamt that Willie
    was here last nicht,
And she widna lat him in.
For she dreamt that Willie
    was here last nicht,
And she widna lat him in.

Go to yer bed my daughter dear,
Lie doon and tak yer rest,
For it's nae the space of half an hour
Since Willie left yer gate.
For it's nae the space of half an hour
Since Willie left yer gate.

It's Maggie rose, put on her clothes
An' to the Clyde went she;
The first step noo that she took in
It took her tae the knee.
The first step noo that she took in
It took her tae the knee.

The next step that she took in
It took her tae the chin,
In the deepest pot in a' the Clyde
She found her Willie in.
In the deepest pot in a' the Clyde
She found her Willie in.

So you have got a cruel mother
And I have got another,
But here we lie in Clyde water
Like sister and like brother.
But here we lie in Clyde water
Like sister and like brother.

Farewell to Lochaber

Words by Allan Ramsay (1686-1757).
The tune is an adaptation of *Limerick's Lamentation* attributed to the Irish harper,
Thomas Connellan (c.1640–1698). This ballad was first published in *Tea Table Miscellany* in 1724.
Arrangement copyright Waltons Publishing

Fare-well to Loch-a-ber, fare-well to my Jean, Where heart-some wi' her I ha'e mo-ny day been, To Loch-a-ber no more, Loch-a-ber no more, We'll may-be re-turn to Loch-a-ber no more. These tears that I shed they are all for my dear, And no' for the dan-gers at-tend-ing on weir, Though borne on rough seas to a far dis-tant shore, May-be to re-turn to Loch-a-ber no more.

Though hurricanes rise, though rise ev'ry wind,
No tempest can equal the storm in my mind;
Though loudest of thunders, on louder waves roar,
There's naething like leavin' my love on the shore.
To leave thee behind me, my heart is sair pain'd;
But by ease that's inglorious no fame can be gain'd;
And beauty and love's the reward of the brave;
And I maun deserve it before I can crave.

Then glory, my Jeanie, maun plead my excuse;
Since honour commands me, how can I refuse?
Without it, I ne'er can have merit for thee,
And losing thy favour, I'd better not be.
I gae then, my lass, to win honour and fame:
And if I should chance to come glorious hame,
I'll bring a heart to thee with love running o'er.
And then I'll leave thee and Lochaber no more.

Allan Ramsay

Come Under My Plaidie

Words by Hector MacNeill (1746–1818). Music by John McGill.

Arrangement copyright Waltons Publishing

Gae 'wa' wi' your plaidie auld Donald, gae 'wa',
I fear nae the cauld blast, the drift or the snaw.
Gae 'wa' wi' your plaidie, I'll no' sit beside ye
Ye micht be my gutcher auld Donald, gae 'wa'.
I'm gaun tae meet Johnnie, he's young and he's bonnie,
He's been at Meg's bridle fu' trig and fu' braw,
Nane dances sae lightly, sae gracefu', sae tightly
His cheeks like the new rose, his brow's like the snaw.

Dear Marion, let that flee stick tae the wa'
Your Jock's but a gowk and has naethin' ava',
The hale o' his pack he has noo on his back
He's thirty and I am but three score and twa.

Be frank noo an' kin'ly I'll busk ye aye finely
Tae kirk or tae merket they'll few gang sae braw,
A bien hoose tae bide in, a chaise for tae ride in,
And flunkies tae tend ye as aft as ye ca'.

My faither aye tellt me, my mither an' a'
Ye'd mak' a guid husband and keep me aye braw.
It's true I lo'e Johnnie, he's young and he's bonnie,
But wae's me I ken he has naethin' ava'.
I hae little tocher, ye've made a guid offer,
I'm noo mair than twenty, my time is but sma'
Sae gie me yer plaidie, I'll creep in beside ye,
I thocht ye'd been aulder than three score and twa.

She crept in avont him beside the stane wa',
Whar' Johnny was list'nin' and heard her tell a'.
The day was appointed, his proud heart it dunted,
And struck 'gainst his side as if bursting in twa.
He wandered home weary, the nicht it was dreary,
And thowless he tint his gait 'mang the deep snaw,
The howlet was screamin' while Johnnie cried, "Women
Wad marry auld nick, if he'd keep them aye braw!"

When the Kye Comes Hame

The words are by James Hogg, the Ettrick Shepherd (1770–1835).
The melody is "The Blaithrie o't", an old air, adapted by Hogg.

Arrangement copyright Waltons Publishing

Come all ye jol-ly shep-herds that whis-tle thro' the glen, I'll
tell ye o' a sec-ret that court-iers din-na ken, What
is the great-est bliss that the tongue o' man can name? 'Tis to
woo a bon-nie las-sie when the kye comes hame.

Chorus
When the kye comes hame, When the kye comes hame, 'Tween the
gloom-in' and the mirk when the kye comes hame.

'Tis not beneath the burgonet nor yet beneath the crown,
'Tis not on couch of velvet nor yet on bed of down;
'Tis beneath the spreading birch in the dell without a name,
Wi' a bonnie, bonnie lassie when the kye comes hame.
   Chorus

Then the eye shines sae bricht the hail soul to beguile,
There's love in ev'ry whisper and joy in ev'ry smile,
O wha would choose a crown wi' its perils and its fame,
And miss a bonnie lassie when the kye comes hame.
   Chorus

See yonder pawky shepherd that lingers on the hill,
His yowes are in the fauld and his lambs are lying still,

Yet he downa gang to rest, for his heart is in a flame
To meet his bonnie lassie when the kye comes hame.
　Chorus

Awa' wi' fame and fortune: what comforts can they gie?
And a' the arts that prey upon man's life and liberty!
Gi'e me the highest joy that the heart o' man can frame:
My bonnie, bonnie lassie when the kye comes hame.
　Chorus

The Rowan Tree

Words by Lady Carolina Nairne.　*Arrangement copyright Waltons Publishing*

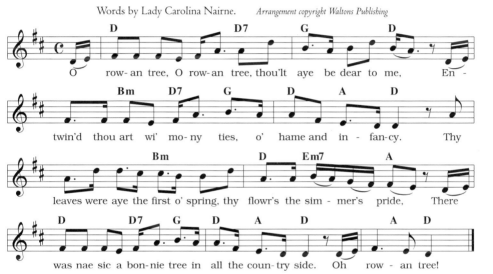

O row-an tree, O row-an tree, thou'lt aye be dear to me,
En-twin'd thou art wi' mo-ny ties, o' hame and in-fan-cy.
Thy leaves were aye the first o' spring, thy flow'rs the sim-mer's pride,
There was nae sic a bon-nie tree in all the coun-try side. Oh row-an tree!

How fair wert thou in simmer time, wi' all thy clusters white.
Now rich and gay thy autumn dress, wi' berries red and bright.
On thy fair stem were mony names which now nae mair I see.
But there engraven on my heart, forgot they ne'er can be.
Oh rowan tree!

We sat aneath thy spreading shade, the bairnies round thee ran.
They pu'd thy bonnie berries red and necklaces they strang.
My mither, oh, I see her still, she smil'd our sports to see,
Wi' little Jeannie on her lap, wi' Jamie at her knee.
Oh rowan tree!

Oh, there arose my father's pray'r in holy evening's calm,
How sweet was then my mither's voice in the martyr's psalm
Now a' are gane! we meet nae mair aneath the rowan tree,
But hallowed thoughts around thee twine o' hame and infancy,
Oh rowan tree!

My Heart's in the Highlands

The first four lines of this song are from an old ballad called "The Strong Walls of Derry". The rest of the words are by Robert Burns. The melody is "Fáilte na Miosg".

Arrangement copyright Waltons Publishing

My heart's in the High-lands, my heart is not here, My heart's in the High - lands, a - cha - sing the deer, A - cha - sing the wild deer, and fol - low-ing the roe, My heart's in the High - lands, wher - ev - er I go. Fare - well to the High - lands, fare - well to the North, The birth - place of val - our, the coun-try of worth! Wher - ev - er I wan - der, wher - ev - er I rove, The hills of the High - lands for ev - er I love.

Farewell to the mountains high cover'd with snow,
Farewell to the straths and green valleys below,
Farewell to the forests and wild-hanging woods,
Farewell to the torrents and loud pouring floods!
My heart's in the Highlands, my heart is not here,
My heart's in the Highlands, a-chasing the deer,
A-chasing the wild deer, and following the roe,
My heart's in the Highlands, wherever I go.

The Skye Boat Song

The words are by Sir Harold Boulton. The first half of the tune is said to be an old sea shanty;
the other half is traditionally attributed to Miss Annie MacLeod. The song refers to Bonnie Prince Charlie,
the Young Pretender, and his escape after defeat at Culloden in 1746 to the island of Skye.

Arrangement copyright Waltons Publishing

Speed bon-nie boat like a bird on the wing, On - ward the sail - ors cry.— Car - ry the lad that's born to be king Ov - er the sea to Skye.— Loud, the winds howl, loud the waves roar, Thun-der - claps rend the air,— Baff - led our foes stand on the shore, Fol-low they will not dare.

Though the waves leap	Many's the man
Soft shall ye sleep;	Fought on that day
Ocean's a royal bed.	Well the claymore could wield,
Rocked in the deep,	When the night came,
Flora will keep	Silently lay
Watch o'er your weary head.	Dead on Culloden's field.
Chorus	Chorus

Burned are our homes,
Exile and death
Scattered the loyal men,
Yet ere the sword
Cool in the sheath
Charlie will come again.
Chorus

O Saw Ye My Dearie?

This song was written by Robert Burns as an alternative to an older song which, in his own words "had more wit than decency". The air appears in Oswald's *Pocket Companion* under the title "Appie McNabb".

Arrangement copyright Waltons Publishing

What says she, my dearie, my Eppie Macnab?
What says she, my dearie, my Eppie Macnab?
She lets thee to wit that she has thee forgot,
And forever disowns thee, her ain Jock Rab.

O, had I ne'er seen thee, my Eppie Macnab!
O, had I ne'er seen thee, my Eppie Macnab!
As light as the air, and as fause as thou's fair,
Thou's broken the heart o' thy ain Jock Rab!

Eppie Macnab

These words were written by Lady Nairne, and are sung to the same air as "O Saw Ye My Dearie".

O mind ye nae, mind ye nae, Eppie Macnab?
It's no sae lang syne yet, O Eppie Macnab,
Sin' your e'en they shone bricht, and your heart it lapt licht,
Gin ye'd seen the shadow o' blythe Jock Rab.

Chorus:
But weary now, weary now's wae Jock Rab,
O weary now, weary now's wae Jock Rab,
My joy and my pride, I lo'ed aye like a bride,
She's fause and forsaken her ain Jock Rab.

O wae worth the lordling, my Eppie Macnab,
O wae worth the lordling, my Eppie Macnab;
His fancy ye'll tine, ye maun nae mair be mine,
And the warld's now a waste to your ain Jock Rab.
   Chorus

An' ye saw yer wee bairnies now, Eppie Macnab,
Your mitherless bairnies now, Eppie Macnab;
They greet and think shame, gin they hear but your name,
And they wring the heart's blude frae your ain Jock Rab.
   Chorus

Lady Carolina Nairne

The Reel o' Stumpie

The first verse can be used as a chorus or sung after the last verse.

Arrangement copyright Waltons Publishing

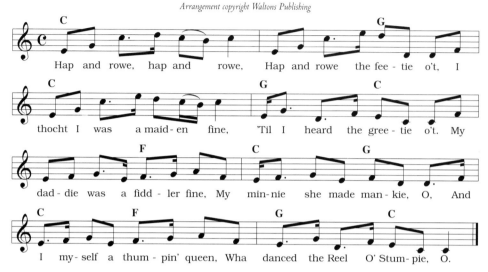

Hap and rowe, hap and rowe, Hap and rowe the fee-tie o't, I thocht I was a maid-en fine, 'Til I heard the gree-tie o't. My dad-die was a fidd-ler fine, My min-nie she made man-kie, O, And I my-self a thum-pin' queen, Wha danced the Reel O' Stum-pie, O.

Dance and sing, dance and sing,
Hey, the merry dancing, O,
And all the love-locks wavin' 'round
And all the bright eyes glancin', O.

The pipes come wi' their gladsome note
And then with dool and dumpie, O,
But the lightest tune to a maiden's foot
Is the gallant Reel o' Stumpie, O.

The gossip cup, the gossip cup
The kimmer clash and caudle, O,
The waning moon, the wanton loon,
The cutty stool and cradle, O.

Douce dames wha hae their bairn-time borne
Sae dinna glower sae glumpie, O,
Cocks love the morn and crows love corn
And maids the Reel o' Stumpie, O.

My Last Farewell to Stirling

Arrangement copyright Waltons Publishing

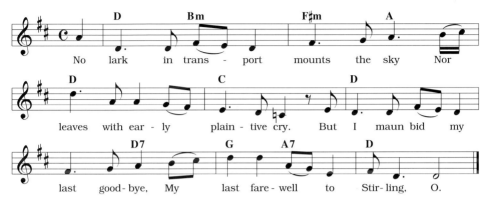

No lark in trans - port mounts the sky Nor
leaves with ear - ly plain - tive cry. But I maun bid my
last good - bye, My last fare - well to Stir - ling, O.

Far awa', my hairt's wi' you,
Our youthful hours on wings they flew;
But I will bid my last adieu,
My last farewell to Stirling, O.

Nae mair I'll meet you in the dark,
Nor gang wi' you to the king's park.
Nor raise the hare oot frae their flap
When I gang far frae Stirling, O.

Nae mair I'll wander through the glen,
Nor disturb the roost o' the pheasant hen,
Nor chase the rabbits to their den,
When I gang far frae Stirling, O.

There's one request before I go,
And that is to my comrades all,
My dog and gun ye'll keep for me,
When I gang far frae Stirling, O.

Noo fare ye weel, my Jeannie dear,
For you I'll shed a bitter tear,
But I hope you'll find some other, dear,
When I am far frae Stirling, O.

Then fare ye weel, for I am bound
For twenty years to Van Dieman's Land.
But speak of me and what I've done,
When I gang far frae Stirling, O.

John Anderson My Jo

The first and last verses are by Robert Burns. The second verse is by William Reed, a Glasgow bookseller.

According to tradition John Anderson was town piper of Kelso, and a bit of a wag.

The tune is written in Queen Elizabeth's Virginal Book 1578.

William Reed, a Glasgow bookseller, inserted the second verse around 1798.

Arrangement copyright Waltons Publishing

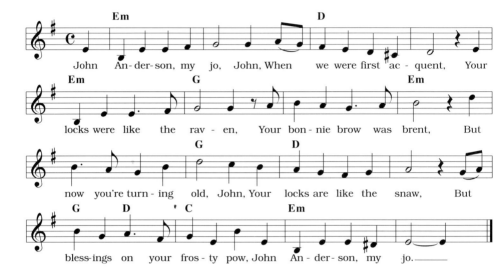

John Anderson, my jo, John, When we were first ac - quent, Your locks were like the rav - en, Your bon - nie brow was brent, But now you're turn - ing old, John, Your locks are like the snaw, But bless-ings on your fros - ty pow, John An - der - son, my jo.

John Anderson, my jo, John,
When Nature first began
To try her canny hand, John,
Her master work was man;
And you amang them a', John
Sae trig from top to toe,
She prov'd to be nae journey work,
John Anderson, my jo.

John Anderson my jo, John,
We clamb the hill the gither;
And mony a canty day, John,
We've had wi' ane anither:
Now we maun totter down, John,
And hand in hand we'll go;
And sleep the gither at the foot,
John Anderson my jo.

John Anderson My Jo

This older version of the song was collected by Robert Burns, and as in the case of some other songs
he put his own more decorous words to it. Suffice it to say that the woman is frustrated,
and that "hurdies fyke" translates as "restless buttocks".

John Anderson, my jo, John,
I wonder what you mean
To lie sae lang in the morning
And sit sae late at e'en.
Ye'll bleer a' your een, John,
And why do you so?
Come sooner to your bed at e'en,
John Anderson, my jo.

John Anderson, my jo, John,
When first that ye began,
Ye had as good a tail-tree
As ony ither man;
But now its waxen wan, John,
And wrinkles to and fro,
I've twa gae-ups for ae gae-down
John Anderson, my jo.

I'm backit like a salmon,
I'm brestit like a swan,
My wame it is down-cod,
My middle ye may span.
Frae my tap-knot to my tae, John,
I'm like the new fa'n snow,
And its a' for your conveniency,
John Anderson, my jo.

O it is a fine thing
To keep out o'er the dyke,
But it is a mickle finer thing
To see your hurdies fyke
To see your hurdies fyke, John,
And hit the rising blow,
It's then I like your chanter pipe,
John Anderson, my jo.

When ye came on before, John
See that ye do your best,
When ye begin to haud me
See that ye grip me fast.
See that ye grip me fast, John,
Until that I cry, Oh!
Your back shall crack or I do that,
John Anderson, my jo.

John Anderson, my jo, John,
Ye're welcome when you please,
It's either in the warm bed,
Or else aboon the claes.
Or ye shall hae the horns, John,
Upon your head to grow,
An that's the cuckold's mallison,
John Anderson, my jo, John.

The Lea Rig

Words by Robert Burns.

Arrangement copyright Waltons Publishing

When o'er the hill the east-ern star Tells bugh-tin time is near, my jo, And ow-sen frae the fur-row'd field, Re - turn sae dowf and wear-ie, O; Down by the burn, where scen-ted birks Wi' dew are hang-ing clear, my jo, I'll meet thee on the lea - rig, My ain kind dear-ie, O.

At midnicht hoor in mirkest glen
I'd rove and ne'er be eerie O,
If thro' that glen I gaed tae thee,
My ain kind dearie O,
And tho' the nicht were ne'er sae wild,
And I were ne'er sae weary O,
I'll meet thee on the lea rig,
My ain kind dearie O.

The hunter lo'es the morning sun,
Tae rouse the mountain deer, my jo,
At noon the fisher taks the glen,
A-doon the burn tae steer, my jo,
But gie tae me the gloamin' grey
It maks my heart sae cheery O,
Tae meet ye on the lea rig,
My ain kind dearie O.

The Road to the Isles

From *Songs of the Hebrides Vol. II* collected by Marjory Kennedy-Fraser and Kenneth Macleod.
Words by Kenneth Macleod.

It's by Shiel water the track is to the west,
By Aillort and by Morar to the sea,
The cool cresses I am thinkin' of for pluck
And bracken for a wink on mother knee.
  Chorus

The blue islands are pullin' me away,
Their laughter puts the leap upon the lame;
The blue islands from the Skerries to the Lewis
Wi' heather honey taste upon each name.
  Chorus

Sally Munro

The *Newry* was wrecked in the Lleyn Peninsula, North Wales, in April, 1830.

Arrangement copyright Waltons Publishing

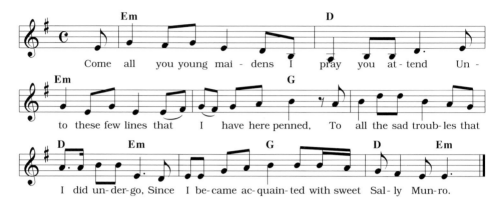

Come all you young mai-dens I pray you at-tend Un-to these few lines that I have here penned, To all the sad troub-les that I did un-der-go, Since I be-came ac-quain-ted with sweet Sal-ly Mun-ro.

James Dickson's my name, I'm a blacksmith by trade,
And in the town of Ayr I was born and bred,
From that town to Belfast I late did go;
'Twas there I got acquainted wi' sweet Sally Munro.

I loved this young lassie as dear as my life;
It was my intention to make her my wife,
But though dearly I loved her, her parents said, "No",
Which caused me to mourn for young Sally Munro.

I unto this lassie a letter did send,
It was by a comrade whom I thought a friend,
But instead of a friend he proved to me a foe
For he ne'er gave the letter to my Sally Munro.

He told her old parents to beware of me:
He said I had a wife in my own country.
Then said her old parents: "Since we've found it so,
He never shall enjoy his sweet Sally Munro".

I said if she'd come to Urie with me,
In spite of her parents there married we'd be.
She said: "No objections have I there to go,
If you only prove constant to Sally Munro".

Here is my hand, love, and here is my heart;
Till death separate us we never shall part.
Next day in a coach we to Urie did go,
And there I got married to young Sally Munro.

It was at Newry Point the ship *Newry* lay,
With four hundred passengers ready for sea,
We both paid our passage to Quebec also;
'Twas there I embarked wi' my Sally Munro.

On the fourteenth of April our ship did set sail,
And hove down the Channel with a sweet pleasant gale,
The parting of friends caused some salt tears to flow,
But I was quite happy wi' my Sally Munro.

When dreading no danger we met with a shock,
When all of a sudden our ship struck a rock,
Three hundred and sixty went all down below,
And in among the number I lost Sally Munro.

Many a man on that voyage lost his life
And children they loved far dearer than life,
Yet I was preserved and my salt tears do flow.
Oh! I mourn when I mind on my Sally Munro.

It was from her parents I stole her away,
Which will check my conscience till my dying day,
But she said: "No objections have I now to go",
And now I'll keep sighing for Sally Munro.

The Road to Dundee

Arrangement copyright Waltons Publishing

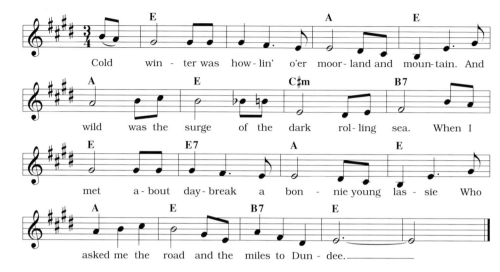

Cold win - ter was how - lin' o'er moor - land and moun - tain. And wild was the surge of the dark rol - ling sea. When I met a - bout day - break a bon - nie young las - sie Who asked me the road and the miles to Dun - dee.

"My young lassie, I canna weel tell ye,
The road and the distance I canna weel gie,
But if you'll permit me to gang a wee bittie,
I'll show you the road and the miles to Dundee".

The lassie consented and gied me her airm,
Not a word did I speir wha the lassie micht be,
She appeared like an angel in feature and form,
As she walked by my side on the road to Dundee.

At length wi' the howe o' Strathmartine behind us
The spires o' the toon in full view we could see,
She said, "Gentle sir, I can never forget ye
For showin' me so far on the road to Dundee.

"This ring and this purse please accept as a token,
And surely there's somethin' that ye can gie me,
That in years to come I'll the laddie remember,
Who showed me the road and the miles to Dundee?"

I took the gold pin frae the scarf on my bosom,
And said, "Tak' ye this, in remembrance o' me",
And bravely I kissed the sweet lips o' the lassie,
And I pairted frae her on the road to Dundee.

So here's tae the lassie; I canna forget her,
And ilka young laddie wha's listenin' to me,
O never be sweir to convey a young lassie,
Though it's only to show her the road to Dundee.

Sae Far Awa

Words by Robert Burns.
Arrangement copyright Waltons Publishing

O, sad and hea-vy should I part But for her sake sae far a-wa, Un - know - ing what my way may thwart, My na - tive land sae far a - wa, Thou that of a' things Ma - ker art, That formed this fair sae far a - wa Gie bo - dy strength, then I'll ne'er start At this my way sae far a-wa!

How true is love to pure desert!
So love to her sae far awa,
And nocht shall heal my bosom's smart
While, Oh, she is sae far awa!

Nane other love, nane other dart
I feel, but hers sae far awa;
But fairer never touch'd a heart
Than hers, the fair sae far awa

The Band o' Shearers

Arrangement copyright Waltons Publishing

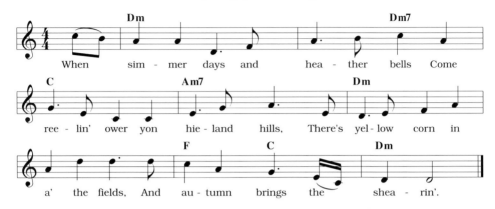

When sim - mer days and hea - ther bells Come ree - lin' ower yon hie - land hills, There's yel - low corn in a' the fields, And au - tumn brings the shea - rin'.

Chorus:
Bonnie lassie, will ye gang
And shear wi' me the whole day lang?
And love will cheer us as we gang
Tae join the band o' shearers.

And gin the weather, it be hot,
I'll cast my cravat and cast me coat,
And we will join the happy lot,
As they gang tae the shearin'.
    Chorus

And gin the thistle be ower strang,
An' pierce your lily, milk white hand,
It's wi' my hook, I'll cut it doon,
As we gang tae the band o' shearers.
    Chorus

An' if the folk that's passing by,
Say there is love 'tween you and I,
An' we will proudly pass them by,
As we gae tae the shearin'.
    Chorus

An' when the shearin' is a' done,
We'll hae some roaring, rantin' fun,
We'll hae some roarin', rantin' fun,
An' forget the toils o' shearin'.

Final chorus:
So bonnie lassie, bricht and fair
Will ye be mine for ever mair?
Gin ye'll be mine, syne I'll be thine
And we'll gang nae mair tae the shearin'.

For the Sake o' Somebody

The "Somebody" in this song is Bonnie Prince Charlie. It is derived from a piece by Allan Ramsay
and was written by Robert Burns for his *Scots Musical Museum*.

Arrangement copyright Waltons Publishing

My heart is sair, I daur - na tell, My heart is sair for Some - bo - dy,

I could wake a win - ter night, For the sake o' Some - bo - dy,

Oh! hon, for Some bo - dy, Oh! hey! for Some - bo - dy,

I could range the world a-round, For the sake o' Some - bo - dy.

Ye powers that smile on virtuous love,
Oh! sweetly smile on Somebody,
Frae ilka danger keep him free,
And send me safe my Somebody;

Oh! hon, for Somebody,
Oh! hey! for Somebody,
I wad do what wad I not,
For the sake o' Somebody.

Flora MacDonald's Lament

The story of Flora MacDonald helping Bonnie Prince Charlie to escape over the sea to Skye with
the Prince dressed as her maid, is the subject of many Jacobite songs. This one is by James Hogg,
the Ettrick Shepherd, to a tune written by Neil Gow Junior.

Arrangement copyright Waltons Publishing

The moorcock that crows on the brows o' Ben Connal,
He kens o' his bed in a sweet mossy hame;
The eagle that soars o'er the cliffs o' Clan Ranald,
Unaw'd and unhunted his eyrie can claim;
The solan can sleep on the shelves of the shore,
The cormorant roost on his rock of the sea;
But ah! there is one whose fate I deplore,
Nor house, ha' nor hame in this country has he;
The conflict is past, and our name is no more,
There's nought left but sorrow for Scotland and me.

The target is torn from the arm of the just,
The helmet is cleft on the brow of the brave;
The claymore forever in darkness must rust,
But red is the sword of the stranger and slave.
The hoof of the horse, and the foot of the proud,
Have trod o'er the plumes on the bonnet of blue;
Why slept the red bolt in the breast of the cloud,
When tyranny revell'd in blood of the true?
Fareweel my young hero, the gallant and good,
The crown of thy fathers is torn from thy brow.

Flora MacDonald

The Laird o' Cockpen

Words by Lady Carolina Nairne (1766-1845); additional verses by Sir Andrew Boswell.
The Laird of Cockpen was a companion-in-arms to Charles II, and was in exile with him in the Netherlands.
The original tune was "When She Came Ben She Bobbit" which appears in a 1692 manuscript.

Arrangement copyright Waltons Publishing

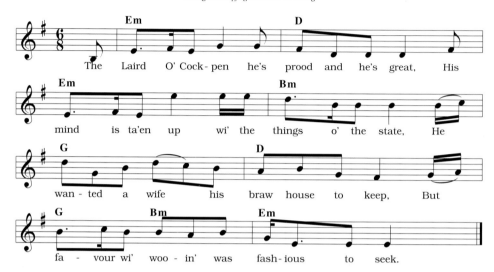

The Laird O' Cock-pen he's prood and he's great, His
mind is ta'en up wi' the things o' the state, He
wan-ted a wife his braw house to keep, But
fa-vour wi' woo-in' was fash-ious to seek.

Now doon by the dykeside a lady did dwell,
At his table head he thocht she'd look well;
MacCleish's ae dochter o' Clavers ha' Lee,
A penniless lass wi' a lang pedigree.

He mounted his mare an' he rade cannily,
An' rapp'd at the yett o' Claver ha' Lee,
"Gae tell mistress Jean to come speedily ben,
She's wanted to speak wi' the Laird o' Cockpen."

Mistress Jean she was makin' the elder flow'r wine,
"What the deil brings the Laird here at sic a like time?"
She put off her apron and on her silk gown,
Her mutch wi' red ribbons, an gae'd awa' doon.

An' when she came ben she bobbit fu' low,
And what was his errand he soon let her know;
Amaz'd was the Laird, when the lady said, "Na!"
An' wi' a laigh curtise she turned awa'.

Dumbfounded was he, but nae sigh did he gie;
He mounted his mare an' he rode cannily;
And aften he thocht, as he gae'd thro' the glen,
She was daft to refuse the Laird o' Cockpen.

And now that the Laird, his exit has made,
Mistress Jean she reflected on what she had said,
"O for ane I'll get better, it's waur I'll get ten,
I was daft tae refuse the Laird O' Cockpen."

The last that the Laird and his Lady were seen
They had gaed arm in arm tae the kirk i' the green.
Now she sits i' the ha' like a weel-tappit' hen
But as yet there's nae chicks ha' appeared in Cockpen.

The White Cockade

Words by Robert Burns.

Arrangement copyright Waltons Publishing

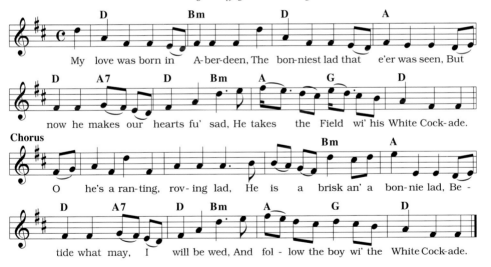

My love was born in A-ber-deen, The bon-niest lad that e'er was seen, But now he makes our hearts fu' sad, He takes the Field wi' his White Cock-ade.

Chorus
O he's a ran-ting, rov-ing lad, He is a brisk an' a bon-nie lad, Be-tide what may, I will be wed, And fol-low the boy wi' the White Cock-ade.

I'll sell my rock, my reel, my tow,
My gude gray mare and hawkit cow;
To buy mysel a tartan plaid,
To follow the boy wi the White Cockade.
Chorus

The Braes of Balquidder

Words by Robert Tannahill.

Arrangement copyright Waltons Publishing

Will you go, las - sie, go To the Braes of Bal - quid - der? Where the blue ber - ries grow 'Mang the bon - nie bloo - ming hea - ther, Where the deer and the rae Light - ly boun - ding to - ge - ther, Spend the long sum - mer day By the braes of Bal - quid - der. Where the deer and the rae Light - ly boun ding to - ge - ther, Spend the long sum - mer day By the braes of Bal - quid - der.

I would twine you a bower
By some silvery fountain,
And deck it all o'er
With flowers from the mountain.
I will range through the wilds
And the deep glens so dreary,
And return wi' their spoils
Tae the bower o' my dearie.

"Oh no sir," she said,
"I'm too young to be your lover;
For my age is scarce sixteen,
And I dare not for my mother.
And beside being so young,
I am afraid you're some deceiver,
That have come to charm me here
By the braes of Balquidder."

Fare you well my pretty fair maid,
Your beauty soon may wither,
I'll deprive you of your chance,
And live happy with some other.
I will roam the wide world over
Till I find a maid of honour,
That will go along with me
To the banks of Balquidder.

"Oh come back, oh come back,
For I think you're no deceiver,
Oh come back, oh come back,
I will never love none other,
I will leave all my friends
Father, mother, sister, brother,
And I will go along with you
To the braes of Balquidder."

Oh now they have gone
To that bonnie highland mountain,
For to view the green fields
Likewise its silvery fountain,
It's there they are united,
And joined in love together,
Spend a long summer day
By the braes of Balquidder.

The Braes of Balquidder

Caller O'u

This song describes how oysters were sold by girls who carried creels of oysters from door to door.
"Caller O'u" means freshly caught oysters. The words and music are by Dr. John Gray.

Arrangement copyright Waltons Publishing

A guid New year to one and a' An' mo-ny may ye see, An'
du-ring a' the years to come O hap-py may ye be.___ An'
may ye ne'er hae cause to mourn, To sigh or shed a tear; To
ane an' a' baith great an' sma' A hear-ty guid New year.

Chorus

A guid New year to one and a' An' mo-ny may ye see, An'
du-ring a' the years to come O hap-py may ye be.___

At night round the ingle sae canty are we,
The oyster lass brings her treat frae the sea,
Wi' music and sang, as time passes by,
We hear in the distance the creel-lassie's cry.
   Chorus

Success to the boatmen at hame and awa',
At kirk and at fair there's nane gaes sae braw,
And lead be their dames, sae blythe-some and fair,
Their voice in the ev'ning is music to hear.
   Chorus

The March o' the Cameron Men

It is thought that this song refers to the 1745 Rising. The Cameron Clan, from Lochaber in the far west of the Highlands of Scotland, was often described as "fiercer than fierceness itself". Donald Cameron of Lochiel was chief of the Cameron Clan at the time and was known as "the gentle Lochiel". He tried to persuade Prince Charlie to return to France and wait for a more favourable opportunity, but when he found the Prince determined to "put all to the hazard", he answered, "Then I will share the fate of my Prince, and so shall every man over whom nature or fortune hath given me any power." He was wounded at Culloden and escaped to France where he commanded a French regiment. He died in 1748.

Arrangement copyright Waltons Publishing

Oh, proudly they walk, but each Cameron knows
He may tread on the heather no more,
But boldly he follows his chief to the field,
Where his laurels were gathered before.
I hear the pibroch etc.

The moon has arisen, it shines on the path
Now trod by the gallant and true;
High, high are their hopes, for their chieftain has said
That whatever men dare, they can do.
I hear the pibroch etc.

A Guid New Year

Words by P. Livingstone. Music by A. Hume.

Arrangement copyright Waltons Publishing

O time flies past, he winna wait,
My friend, for you or me,
He works his wonders day by day,
And onward still doth flee.
O wha can tell when ilka ane,
I see sae happy here,
Will meet again and merry be
Anither guid New Year?
  Chorus

We twa ha'e baith been happy lang.
We ran about the braes.
In yon wee cot beneath the tree,
We spent our early days.

We ran about the burnie's side,
The spot will aye be dear,
An' those that used to meet us there,
We'll think on mony a year.
  Chorus

Noo let us hope our years may be
As guid as they ha'e been,
And trust we ne'er again may see,
The sorrows we ha'e seen.
And let us wish that ane an' a'
Our friends baith far an' near,
May aye enjoy in times to come
A hearty guid New year!
Chorus

Bonnie Dundee

The most prominent figure in the first Jacobite rebellion was "Bonnie Dundee", John Graham, Earl of Claverhouse. He was killed in his victory at Killikrankie (July 1689) and shortly after the resistance was defeated at the battle of Dunkeld. Words by Sir Walter Scott.

Arrangement copyright Waltons Publishing

Dundee he is mounted he rides up the street,
The bells are rung backward, the drums they are beat,
But the provost douce man said just e'en let him be,
The guid town is well quit o' that deil o' Dundee.
    Chorus

There are hills beyond Pentland and lands beyond Forth,
Be there lords in the Lowlands they've Chiefs in the North,
There are wild Du-nie-was-sals, three thousand times three
Will cry "Hoi!" for the bonnet of Bonnie Dundee.
    Chorus

Then away to the hills to the caves to the rocks,
Ere I own a usurper I'll crouch with the fox,
And tremble false Whigs in the midst of your glee,
You have not seen the last of my bonnet an' me.
    Chorus

My Laddie Sits Ower Late

Hogg published this song in his *Jacobites Relics* with the following note:
"I got the original of these verses from my friend Mr. Neil Gow, who told me they were a translation
from the Gaelic, but so rude that he could not publish them...on which I versified them anew,
and made them a great deal better without altering one sentiment."
Arrangement copyright Waltons Publishing

My lad-die sits ow-er late up, My hin-ny sits ow-er late up, My
dear-ie sits ow-er late up, Be-twixt the pint pot and the cup.

Hey, Johnny, come hame to your bairn,
Hey, Johnny, come hame to your bairn,
Hey, Johnny, come hame to your bairn,
Wiv a rye loaf under your airm.

He addles three-ha'pence a week,
That's nobbut a farthing a day;
He sits wiv his pipe in his cheek,
And fiddles his money away.

My laddie is never the near,
My hinny is never the near,
And when I cry out, "Laddie, come hame,"
He calls oot again for mair beer.

Bonnie Wee Jeannie McColl

This song was popular as a music hall song in the early twentieth century.

Arrangement copyright Waltons Publishing

The very first nicht I met her, she was awfy, awfy shy,
The rain cam' pourin' doon, but she was happy, so was I.
We ran like mad for shelter, an' we landed up a stair,
The rain cam' poorin' oot o' ma breeks, but och I didna care:
For she's ....
    Chorus

Noo I've wad my Jeannie, an' bairnies we have three,
Two dochters and a braw wee lad, that sits upon my knee.
They're richt wee holy terrors, an' they're never still for lang,
But they sit an' listen every nicht, while I sing to them this sang:
Oh it's ....
    Chorus

Bonnie George Campbell

This ballad is also known as "Bonnie James Campbell". A variation appeared in Scott's Scottish Songs (1795-1806). The ballad is probably a lament for one of two cousins, Archibald or James Campbell who both died in the battle of Glenlivet on October 3, 1594. A "John Campbell" version concerns the murder of Sir John Campbell of Calder by another Campbell in 1591.

Arrangement copyright Waltons Publishing

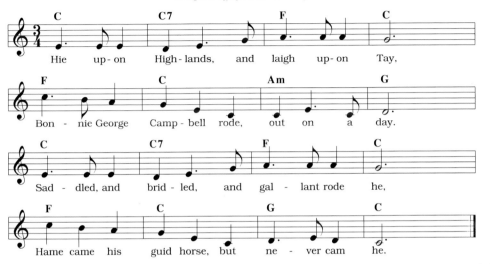

Hie up-on High-lands, and laigh up-on Tay,
Bon - nie George Camp - bell rode, out on a day.
Sad - dled, and brid - led, and gal - lant rode he,
Hame came his guid horse, but ne - ver cam he.

Out cam his mother, dear, greeting fu sair,
And out cam his bonnie bryde, riving her hair.
"The meadow lies green the corn is unshorn
But bonnie George Campbell will never return".

Saddled and bridled and booted rode he,
A plume in his helment, a sword at his knee.
But toom cam his saddle, all bloody to see,
Oh, hame cam his guid horse, but never cam he.

Hie upon the Highlands, and laigh upon Tay,
Bonnie George Campbell rode, out on a day.
Saddled and bridled and gallant rode he,
Hame came his guid horse, but never cam he.

O where is he lying, tell me but where?
Is he drowned in the Yarrow, or lost in Quhair?
O vain are thy wailings, the echoes reply,
Bonnie George Campbell, ye'll see him nae mair.

A Scottish Emigrant's Farewell

Words & music by Alexander Hume.

Arrangement copyright Waltons Publishing

Fare - weel, fare-weel my na - tive hame, Thy lone - ly hills an'
heath clad moun-tains, Fare - weel thy fields o' sto - ried fame, Thy
lea - fy shaws and spark - ling foun-tains, Nae mair I'll climb the
Pent-lands steep, Nor wan - der by the Esk's clear ri - ver, I seek a hame far
o'er the deep, My na - tive land, Fare - weel for - ev - er.

Thou land wi' love and freedom crown'd,
In ilk wee cot an' lordly dwellin',
May manly hearted youths be found,
And maids in ev'ry grace excellin'.
The land where Bruce and Wallace wight,
For freedom fought in days o' danger,
Never crouch'd to proud usurpin' right,
But foremost stood, wrongs stern avenger.

Tho' far frae thee, my native shore,
An' toss'd on life's tempestuous ocean;
My heart, aye Scottish to the core,
Shall cling to thee wi' warm devotion,
An' while the wavin' heather grows,
An' onward rows the windin' river,
The toast be, "Scotland's broomy knowes,
Her mountains, rocks an' glens forever".

The Bonnie Lass of Fenario

Arrangement copyright Waltons Publishing

As we marched down to Fe - na - ri - o, As we marched down to Fe - na - ri - o, Our cap-tain fell in love with a la - dy like a dove, And the name she was called was pre - tty Peg- gy - o.

Come go along with me, Pretty Peggy-o,
Come go along with me, Pretty Peggy-o,
In coaches you will ride with your true love by your side,
Just as grand as any lady in the areo.

What would your mother think, Pretty Peggy-o?
What would your mother think, Pretty Peggy-o?
What would your mother think for to hear the guineas clink,
And the soldiers all a marching before you o?

You're the man that I adore, Handsome Willi-o,
You're the man that I adore, Handsome Willi-o,
You're the man that I adore, but your fortune is too low.
I'm afraid my mother would be angry-o.

Come a tripping down the stairs, Pretty Peggy-o,
Come a tripping down the stairs, Pretty Peggy-o,
Come a tripping down the stair, tie up your yellow hair,
Bid a last farewell to handsome Willy-o.

If ever I return, Pretty Peggy-o,
If ever I return, Pretty Peggy-o,
If ever I return, the city I will burn,
And destroy all the ladies in the areo.

Our captain, he is dead, Pretty Peggy-o,
Our captain, he is dead, Pretty Peggy-o,
Our captain he is dead, he died for a maid,
And he's buried in Louisiana county-o.

Roslin Castle

The air to "Roslin Castle" was attributed to James Oswald. Although it appears in his *Curious Collection of Scots Tunes*, he had not marked it as his tune. It had appeared in a previous collection by William McGibbon as *The House of Glams*. The words were written by Richard Hewitt of Cumberland, who was employed as a guide to Dr. Blacklock, who was blind. Blacklock was so impressed by the boy that he educated him. He subsequently became secretary to Lord Milton and died in 1764.

Arrangement copyright Waltons Publishing

'Twas in the sea-son of the year, When all things gay and sweet ap-pear, That Co-lin with the morn-ing ray A-rose and sung his ru-ral lay, Of Nan-ny's charms the shep-herd sung, The hills and dales with Nan-ny rung, And Ros-lin cast-tle heard the swain, And e-cho'd back the cheer-ful strain.

Awake, sweet muse! the breathing spring
With rapture warms, awake and sing!
Awake, and join the vocal throng
Who hail the morning with a song.
To Nanny raise the cheerful lay,
O bid her haste and come away;
In sweetest smiles herself adorn,
And add new graces to the morn.

O hark, my love, on every spray
Each feather'd warbler tunes his lay;
'Tis beauty fires the ravish'd throng,
And love inspires the melting song.
Then let my raptur'd notes arise,
For beauty darts from Nanny's eyes,
And love my rising bosom warms,
And fills my soul with sweet alarms.

O come, my love! thy Colin's lay
With rapture calls, O come away!
Come, while the Muse this wreath shall twine
Around that modest brow of thine.
O hither haste, and with thee bring
That beauty blooming like the spring,
Those graces that divinely shine,
And charm this ravish'd breast of mine.

Roslin Castle 1779

Roslin Castle (1304) is situated on the north bank of the river Esk not far from Edinburgh.
Roslin (ross [from the gaelic] = promontory, lyn = pool) has been in the hands of the St. Clair family since 1070.
It is famous for the Battle of Roslin when in 1303 the Scots, with only 10,000 men, defeated the English with a strength of 30,000.
Over the centuries it has ceased to be used as a castle, but a mansion has been built within the ruins.
More famous is the nearby Roslin Chapel founded in 1446 by William St. Clair,
and featured in the best selling novel The Da Vinci Code.

The Cooper o' Dundee

Collected by Robert Burns.

Arrangement copyright Waltons Publishing

Ye coo-pers and hoo-pers, at-tend to my dit-ty, I sing o' a coo-per wha dwelt in Dun-dee; This young man he was baith am-'rous and wit-ty, He pleased the fair maids wi the blink o' his e'e. He was nae a coo-per, a com-mon tub-hoo-per, The most o' his trade lay in pleas-in' the fair; He hoopt them, he coopt them, he bort them, he plugt them, An' a' sent for San-dy when out o' re-pair.

For a twelvemonth or sae this youth was respected,
An' he was as busy, as weel he could be;
But bus'ness increased so that some were neglected,
Which ruined trade in the town o' Dundee.
A baillie's fair daughter had wanted a coopin',
And Sandy was sent for, as oft time was he;
He yerkt her sae hard that she sprung an end-hoopin'
Which banish'd poor Sandy frae bonnie Dundee.

Comin' Thro' the Rye

Various versions of this song appeared in a collection by Thomas Mansfield in 1770/1780.
This version is by Robert Burns. The air is "O Dinna Ask Me gin I Lo'e Thee".

Arrangement copyright Waltons Publishing

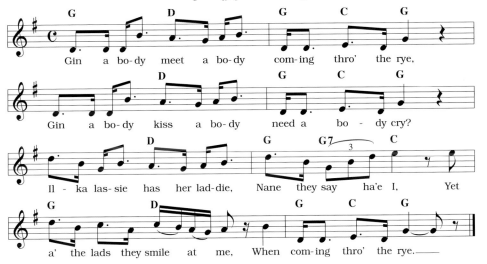

Gin a body meet a body coming thro' the rye,
Gin a body kiss a body need a body cry?
Il - ka las-sie has her lad-die, Nane they say ha'e I, Yet
a' the lads they smile at me, When com-ing thro' the rye.

Gin a body meet a body
Comin' frae the well,
Gin a body kiss a body
Need a body tell?
Ilka lassie—etc.

Gin a body meet a body
Comin' frae the town,
Gin a body kiss a body
Need a body frown?
Ilka lassie—etc.

'Mang the train there is a swain
I dearly lo'e myself,
But what his name or whaur his hame
I dinna care to tell.
Ilka lassie—etc.

Coorie Doon

Words and music by Matt McGinn. *Copyright Appleseed Music, Inc.*

Chorus

There's darkness doon the mine, my darling,
Darkness, dust and damp,
But we must have our heat, our light,
Our fire and our lamp.
   Chorus

Your daddy coories doon, my darling,
Doon in a three foot seam,
So you can coorie doon, my darling,
Coorie doon and dream.
   Chorus

For A' That and A' That

The words are by Robert Burns. Beranger, the Burns of France, said that this was
"a song not for an age, but for an eternity".

Arrangement copyright Waltons Publishing

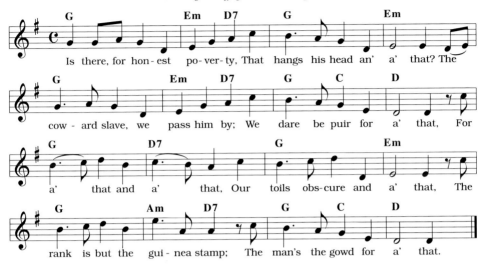

Is there, for hon-est po-ver-ty, That hangs his head an' a' that? The
cow-ard slave, we pass him by; We dare be puir for a' that, For
a' that and a' that, Our toils obs-cure and a' that, The
rank is but the gui-nea stamp; The man's the gowd for a' that.

What though on hamely fare we dine,
Wear hoddin grey, an' a' that?
Gie fools their silks, and knaves their wine,
A man's a man, for a' that.
For a' that, an' a' that,
Their tinsel show an' a' that,
The honest man, though e'er sae poor,
Is king o' men for a' that.

Ye see yon birkie ca'd a lord
Wha struts an' stares an' a' that,
Tho' hundreds worship at his word,
He's but a coof for a' that.
For a' that, an' a' that,
His ribband, star and a' that,
The man o' independent mind
He looks an' laughs at a' that.

A prince can mak' a belted knight,
A marquise, duke, an' a' that,
But an honest man's aboon his might,
Gude faith, he maunna fa' that.
For a' that, an' a' that,
Their dignities an' a' that,
The pith o' sense an' pride o' worth
Are higher rank than a' that.

Then let us pray, that come it may,
As come it will for a' that,
That Sense and Worth, o'er a' the earth
Shall bear the gree an' a' that.
For a' that, an' a' that,
It's coming yet for a' that,
That man to man, the world o'er
Shall brithers be for a' that.

Ye Gowden Vanitee

Arrangement copyright Waltons Publishing

There was a gal-lant ship, and a gal-lant ship was she Eek-ee-dle-ee And the
Low-lands low, And she was called ye *Gow-den Van-it-ee,* As she
sail'd to the Low-lands low. She had-na' sail'd a league, a
league but on-ly three, Eek-ee-dle-ee and the Low-lands low, Till
she fell in wi' a French Gal-lie, as she sail'd to the Low-lands low.

Then up spoke the captain, and up spoke he, Eek- .... etc.
"Oh! wha'll sink for me yon blessed French Gallie?" As she .... etc.

Then up spoke the cabin boy, and up spoke he, Eek- .... etc.
"What will ye gie me if I sink yon French Gallie?" As she .... etc.

Then up spoke the captain, and up spoke he, Eek- .... etc.
"I'll gie ye lands and houses in the North Countree," As she .... etc.

"Then roll me up ticht in a black bull's skin, Eek- .... etc.
And throw me ower deck board, sink I or swim." As she .... etc.

They've rolled him up ticht in a black bull's skin, Eek- .... etc.
And thrown him ower deck board sink he or swim. As she .... etc.

Then a-down, and a-down, and a-down sunk he, Eek- .... etc.
And he swam up to the French Gallie. As she .... etc.

Now some were playin' cards, an' some were playin' dice, Eek- .... etc.
Then he took out an instrument bored thirty holes in a trice. As she .... etc.

Then some they ran wi' cloaks and some they ran wi' caps, Eek- .... etc.
But they tried a' in vain to stop the salt water draps. As she .... etc.

Then aroond, and aroond, and aroond went she, Eek- .... etc.
And she went down to the bottom of the sea. As she .... etc.

Then aroond, and aroond, and aroond swam he, Eek- .... etc.
Till he came up to the Gowden Vanitee, As she .... etc.

"Throw me oot a rope and pu' me up on board, Eek- .... etc.
And prove unto me as guid as your word." As you .... etc.

"We'll no' throw you oot a rope nor pu' you up on board, Eek- .... etc.
Nor prove unto you as guid as our word." As we .... etc.

Then up spoke the cabin boy, and up spoke he, Eek- .... etc.
"Hang me if I don't serve you as I served the French Gallie." As she .... etc.

So they threw him oot a rope and pu'ed him up on board, Eek- .... etc.
And proved unto him far better than their word. As they .... etc.

The Land o' the Leal

Lady Nairne wrote the words when the only child of her friend, Mrs. Archibald Campbell Colquhoun (who had been a lover of Sir Walter Scott at one time) died. The air "Now the Day Dawis" is an ancient hunting song and was mentioned by Gawin Douglas, Bishop of Dunkeld in 1513.

Arrangement copyright Waltons Publishing

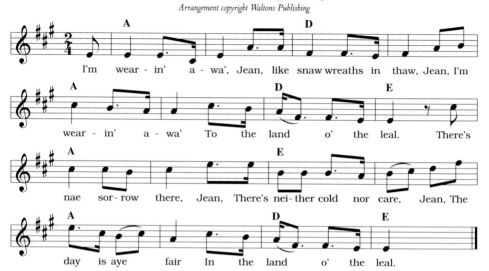

I'm wear-in' a-wa', Jean, like snaw wreaths in thaw, Jean, I'm wear-in' a-wa' To the land o' the leal. There's nae sor-row there, Jean, There's nei-ther cold nor care, Jean, The day is aye fair In the land o' the leal.

Our bonnie bairnie's there, Jean,
She was baith gude and fair, Jean,
And oh! we grudg'd her sair,
To the land o' the leal.
But sorrow's sel' wears past, Jean,
And joy's a-comin' fast, Jean,
The joy that's aye to last, Jean,
In the land o' the leal.

Sae dear that joy was bought, Jean,
Sae free the battle fought, Jean,
That sinfu' man ere brought, Jean,
To the land o' the leal.
My soul langs to be free, Jean,
Then dry that glist'ning e'e, Jean,
And angels beckon me
To the land o' the leal.

Oh! haud ye leal and true, Jean,
Your day it's wearin' thro', Jean,
And I'll welcome you
To the land o' the leal.
Now fare ye weel, my ain Jean,
This warld's care is vain, Jean,
We'll meet and aye be fain Jean,
In the land o' the leal.

The Calton Weaver

Calton is a district of Glasgow which used to be famous for its weaver's workshops.

Arrangement copyright Waltons Publishing

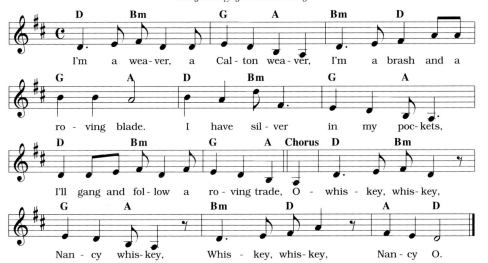

As I cam in by Glesca city,
Nancy Whiskey I chanced to smell,
I gaed in, sat doon beside her,
Seven lang years I lo'ed her well.
   Chorus

The mair I kissed her the mair I lo'ed her,
The mair I kissed her the mair she smiled,
An' I forgot my mither's teaching,
Nancy soon had me beguiled.
   Chorus

I woke early in the morning,
To slake my drouth it was my need,
I tried to rise but I wasna able,
Nancy had me by the heid.
   Chorus

C'wa, landlady whit's the lawin?
Tell me whit there is to pay.
Fifteen shillings is the reckoning,
Pay me quickly and go away.
   Chorus

As I went oot by Glesca city,
Nancy Whiskey I chanced to smell,
I gaed in drank four and sixpence,
A't was left was a crooked scale.
   Chorus

I'll gang back to the Calton weaving
I'll surely mak the shuttles fly
I'll mak mair at the Calton weaving
Than ever I did in a roving way.
   Chorus

Come all ye weavers, Calton weavers,
A' ye weavers where e'er ye be,
Beware of whiskey, Nancy Whiskey,
She'll ruin you as she ruined me.
   Chorus

The Battle o' Stirling

This song was written by William Sinclair to a marching tune composed by J. Marquis Chisholm.
It commemorates William Wallace's victory over King Edward I of England at the
Battle of Stirling Bridge in 1297.

Arrangement copyright Waltons Publishing

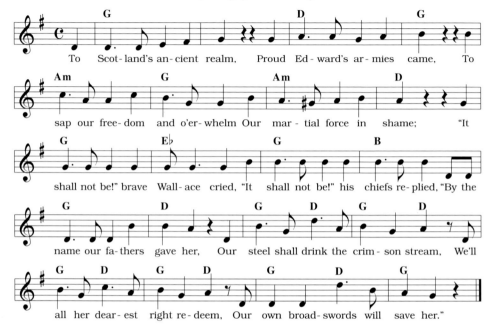

To Scot-land's an-cient realm, Proud Ed-ward's ar-mies came, To
sap our free-dom and o'er-whelm Our mar-tial force in shame; "It
shall not be!" brave Wall-ace cried, "It shall not be!" his chiefs re-plied, "By the
name our fa-thers gave her, Our steel shall drink the crim-son stream, We'll
all her dear-est right re-deem, Our own broad-swords will save her."

With hopes of triumph flush'd,
The squadrons hurried o'er
Thy Bridge Kildean, and heaving rush'd
Like wild waves to the shore.
"They come, they come!" was the gallant cry,
"They come, they come!" was the loud reply.
O strength thou gracious giver,
By love and freedom's stainless faith,
We'll dare the darkest night of death,
We'll drive them back forever.

All o'er the waving broom,
In chivalry and grace,
Shone England's radiant spear and plume
By Stirling's rocky base.
And stretching far beneath the view,
Proud Cressingham, thy banners flew.
When like a torrent rushing,
O God! from right and left the flame,
Of Scottish swords like lightning came,
Great Edward's legions crushing.

High praise, ye gallant band,
Who in the face of day,
With daring hearts and fearless hands
Have cast your chains away.
The foemen fell on ev'ry side,
In crimson hues the Forth was dyed.
Bedew'd with blood the heather,
While cries triumphant shook the air,
Thus shall we do, shall we dare,
Wherever Scotsmen gather!

I'll Lay Ye Doon, Love

Arrangement copyright Waltons Publishing

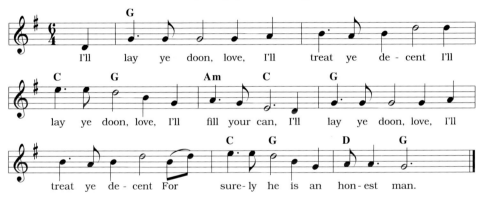

As I walked oot on a summer evenin'
Doon by the water and the pleasant strand,
And as I was walkin, I heard them talkin'
Sayin', "Surely he is an honest man".

I hae travelled far frae Inverney,
Aye, and doon as far as Edinburgh toon,
And it's I maun gae, love, and travel further,
But when I come back, I will lay ye doon.

I maun leave ye noo, love, but I'll return
Tae ye my love and I'll tak' your hand,
Then no more I'll roam frae ye my love,
Nae mair tae walk on a foreign strand.

'Twas Within a Mile o' Edinburgh

Words by Thomas D'Urfey (1653–1723). Music by James Hook.

Arrangement copyright Waltons Publishing

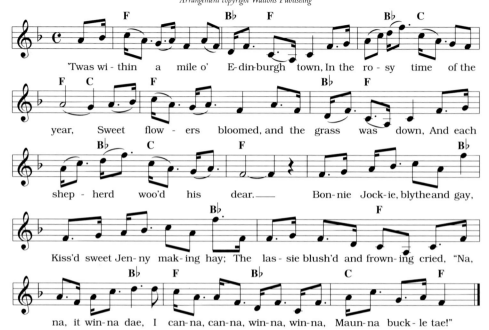

'Twas wi-thin a mile o' E-din-burgh town, In the ro-sy time of the year, Sweet flow-ers bloomed, and the grass was down, And each shep-herd woo'd his dear.— Bon-nie Jock-ie, blythe and gay, Kiss'd sweet Jen-ny mak-ing hay; The las-sie blush'd and frown-ing cried, "Na, na, it win-na dae, I can-na, can-na, win-na, win-na, Maun-na buck-le tae!"

Jockie was a wag that never wad wed,
Though lang he had followed the lass;
Contented she earned and ate her brown bread,
And merrily turned up the grass.
Bonnie Jockie, blythe and free,
Won her heart right merrily,
Yet still she blush'd and frowning cried,
"Na, Na, it winna do;
I canna, canna, winna, winna
Maunna buckle tae."

But when he vow'd he wad make her his bride,
Though his flocks and herds were not few,
She gi'ed him her hand and a kiss beside,
And vow'd she'd forever be true,
Bonnie Jockie, blythe and free,
Won her heart right merrily;
At kirk she no more frowning cried;
"Na, Na, it winna do;
I canna, canna, winna, winna
Maunna buckle tae."

The Blue Bells of Scotland

Words by James Smith. Music ascribed to Mrs. Jordan.

Arrangement copyright Waltons Publishing

Oh fair are the wild flow'rs in ma-ny a for-eign vale,—— And sweet is their frag-rance wide waf-ted on the gale;—— But fair-er far than all that bloom in myr-tle breath-ing dells, Are the gems of old Sco-tia, her wav-ing sweet blue bells.——

When far from her bosom her sons and daughters roam,
To seek from the stranger a country and a home,
How oft the tears unbidden flow as mem'ry fondly dwells
On the gems of old Scotia, her waving, sweet blue bells.

O long may they flourish in all their blooming pride,
On hill, heath and valley and hoary mountain side,
For nought on nature's summer robe in loveliness excels
The gems of old Scotia, her waving, sweet blue bells.

This is an older version of the song. The first line of each verse is sung twice:

Oh where, tell me where, is your Highland laddie gone?
He's gone wi' streaming banners where noble deeds are done,
And it's oh, in my heart I wish him safe at home.

Oh where, tell me where, did your Highland laddie dwell?
He dwelt in Bonnie Scotland, where blooms the sweet blue bell,
And it's oh, in my heart I lo'ed my laddie well.

Oh what, tell me what, does your Highland laddie wear?
A bonnet with a lofty plume, and on his breast a plaid,
And it's oh, in my heart I lo'ed my Highland lad.

Oh what, tell me what, if your Highland laddie's slain?
Oh no, true love will be his guard and bring him safe again,
For it's oh, my heart would break if my Highland lad were slain.

The Four Marys

Arrangement copyright Waltons Publishing

Arise, arise, Mary Hamilton,
Arise and come wi' me,
There is a wedding in Glasgow town,
This night we'll go and see.

She put nae on her robes of black,
Nor yet her robes of brown,
But she put on her gown of white
Tae ride into Glasgow town.

And as she rode into Glasgow town
The city for to see,
The bailiff's wife and the provost's wife
Cried, "Ach and alack for thee."

Oh, often hae I dressed my Queen
And put on her braw silk gown,
But all the thanks I've got tonight,
Is to be hanged in Glasgow Town.

Oh, often hae I dressed my Queen
And put gold in her hair,
But noo I've gotten my reward,
The gallows tae be my share.

For little did my mother think
When first she cradled me,
The lands I was to tread in
Or the death I was tae dee.

Oh, happy, happy is the maid,
That's born of beauty free,
It was my dimplin' rosy cheeks
That's been the doom of me.

"Cast off, cast off my gown," she cried,
"But let my petticoats be,
And tie a napkin around my face,
The gallows I would not see.

"And all you bonnie sailors
That sail across the sea,
Ne'er tell my father or mother
But that I'm across the sea."

Last night there were four Marys
Tonight there'll be but three:
There was Mary Seaton and Mary Beaton
And Mary Carmichael and me.

Glossary

aboon – above

acquent – acquainted

addles – earns

ae – one, only

affa – awful

ane – a, an, one

auld – old

auld-warld cracks – old world stories

ava' – at all

aye – always

bairn – child

baith – both

baw-bee – halfpenny

bear the gree – take first place

ben – in, inward, best room in house

bien – pleasant, cosy, well off

birkie – person

birk – birch

blude – blood

bobbit – bobbed, becked, danced

brae – hill

braw – fine, well-dressed

brent – smooth

buckle – join, marry, dress

bughtin time – time to bring sheep in

burn – stream

busk – adorn, dress neatly

ca'd – called

canna – can not

cannie – quiet, cautious, gentle, skillful

canny – skillful

canty – comfortable, merry

caudle – cuddle

cauld stanney grun' – cold, stony ground

coof – fool, idle/worthless fellow

Coorie doon – snuggle down

corrie – a hollow on the side of a mountain

cot – cottage

creel – basket

cromack – walking staff

curtise – curtsy

cutty stool – stool of repentance in a church

dae – do

daffin – romp

deil – devil

dinna – don't

dochter – daughter

dool and dumpie – short heavy steps

douce – grave, respectable

dowf – spiritless

downa – cannot

dunted – thumped

eerie – scared, gloomy

fain – fond, happy

farthing – one quarter of an old penny

fashious – troublesome

fa' – fault

fauld – fold

fause – false

feetie – little feet

frae – from

gae – go

gang – go

gie – give

gin – if

gloaming – twilight

gowd – gold

gowk – fool

greetie – little cry

greet – cry, weep

grudg'd her sair – missed her sorely

gutcher – grandfather

hail – whole

hamely – homely, humble

hap and rowe – move and turn

haud – hold

hawkit – streaked with white

hinny – honey

hoddin grey – coarse wool

howe – a hollow, low lying ground

howlet – owl, owlet

ilk, ilka – every

ingle – fireside
jo – sweetheart
ken – know
kimmer clash – chat
kirk – church
knowe – hill, hilltop
kye – cows;
laigh – low
lea – grassland, pasture, unploughed
leal – loyal, faithful, true
loon – young fellow
mair – more
malison – malediction, curse
mankie – type of woollen cloth
maun – must
mauna – must not
mavis – thrush
mirk – dark
mutch – cap
nane – none
nobbut – only
nocht – nothing
noo – now
ould – old
ower – too
owsen – oxen
pawky – sly
pouther'd – powdered
pow – head
quean – young woman
rae – roe (deer)
rashes – rushes
rickle o' banes – heap of bones

rig – a strip of land associated with a croft
sae – so, so it is
shaws – wooded dells
shearin' – reaping
sic – such
solan – gannet
sookin – sucking
speir – ask
sweir – reluctant
syne, sin, seen – then, next
tae – to, too
tapsalteerie – topsy-turvy
thocht – thought
thowless – ineffectual
thrifty – piggy-bank
tine – lose
tint his gait – lost his way
tocher – dowry
toom – empty
trig – fine, smart
twae – two
wae – sorrowful
warldly – worldly
waur – worse
wearin' awa'– dying
wears past – passes slowly
weir – war
wha – who
wight – valiant
winna – will not
wit – realise
yett – gate
yowes – ewes